Greatest of All Time College Sports

G.O.A.T. College Football Teams

Diane Lindsey Reeves

Lerner Publications ◆ Minneapolis

Stats in this book are accurate through the 2024 college football season.

Lerner Publications Company
An imprint of Lerner Publishing Group, Inc.
241 First Avenue North
Minneapolis, MN 55401 USA

For reading levels and more information, look up this title at www.lernerbooks.com.

Main body text set in Aptifer Sans LT Pro.
Typeface provided by Linotype.

Library of Congress Cataloging-in-Publication Data

Names: Reeves, Diane Lindsey, 1959–author.
Title: G.O.A.T. college football teams / Diane Lindsey Reeves.
Other titles: Greatest of all time college football teams
Description: Minneapolis : Lerner Publications, [2026] | Series: Lerner Sports. Greatest of all time college sports | "Stats in this book are accurate through the 2023-2024 college football season"—T.p. verso. | Includes bibliographical references and index. | Audience: Ages 7–11 years | Audience: Grades 2–3 | Summary: "The greatest college football teams of all time have traditions of winning year after year. Find out how they do it, meet their greatest players, relive their biggest moments, and create your own G.O.A.T. list"—Provided by publisher.
Identifiers: LCCN 2024054562 (print) | LCCN 2024054563 (ebook) | ISBN 9798765668566 (lib. bdg.) | ISBN 9798765684184 (pbk.) | ISBN 9798765677773 (epub)
Subjects: LCSH: Football—United States—History. | College sports—United States—History. | Football teams—Ratings and rankings—United States.
Classification: LCC GV959.5 .R44 2026 (print) | LCC GV959.5 (ebook) | DDC 796.332/6309—dc23/eng/20250118

LC record available at https://lccn.loc.gov/2024054562
LC ebook record available at https://lccn.loc.gov/2024054563

Manufactured in the United States of America
1-1011967-53824-4/23/2025

TABLE OF CONTENTS

University of Alabama coach Bear Bryant (center right) *watches his team play.*

Touchdown Kings

College football teams don't get much better than the University of Alabama in 1979. The team finished the season with a 12–0 record and were national champs for the sixth time. Like most great teams, their success was due to excellent coaching, amazing players, and a lot of hard work. Alabama's coach was the legendary Bear Bryant. His star players included quarterback Steadman Shealy and running backs Steve Whitman and Major Ogilvie.

Alabama has had its ups and downs. Coaches have come and gone. Some years the roster is stronger than others. But once the seed of greatness takes root in a football program, winning becomes expected. Each year, the team works extra hard to live up to its history.

Alabama scores a touchdown in the 2021 national title game. They beat Ohio State 52–24.

FACTS AT A GLANCE

- The University of Michigan has the most wins in college football history. They have racked up 1,012 victories since their first season in 1879.
- Every University of Nebraska home game since 1962 has been sold out.
- The University of Oklahoma holds the record for the longest winning streak. They won 47 wins in a row from 1953 to 1957.
- At least one player from the University of Southern California (USC) has been chosen in the National Football League (NFL) draft for a record-breaking 69 years in a row.

Over the years, college football rules have changed in ways that make the game safer, fairer, and more fun to watch. One recent change aims to speed up the time between plays. It allows coaches to speak directly to some players through radios in their helmets.

Modern college football teams can use up to 18 computer tablets to watch and rewatch plays during games. This lets coaches view the game from different angles. It helps them plan strategy and coach players.

For more than 100 years, colleges could only offer student athletes scholarships. But college football teams in the US earn more than a billion dollars a year. Recent rule changes allow some of that money to go to the players. College athletes can also profit from the use of their name, image, and likeness in ads, on jerseys, and in other places.

The greatest of all time (G.O.A.T.) college football teams highlighted in this book have long histories of success. They have had some of the best players and coaches in the game. Do you agree with the order of the teams? You'll have a chance to pick your own G.O.A.T. teams at the end. Let's play football!

Quarterback Arch Manning of the Texas Longhorns earned millions of dollars playing for the team.

NO. 10

Louisiana State's Joe Burrow passes the ball against the Oklahoma Sooners in the 2019 Peach Bowl.

LOUISIANA STATE UNIVERSITY

The Louisiana State University (LSU) Tigers made football history in 2019. They went 15–0 and won the Southeastern Conference (SEC) title against Georgia. LSU creamed Oklahoma 63–28 in the Peach Bowl. To top it off, LSU beat Clemson, the defending champions, for the national title.

In 2019, senior quarterback Joe Burrow broke a National Collegiate Athletic Association (NCAA) record with 60 touchdown passes. His 5,671 passing yards ranked third in college history at the time. He won the Heisman Trophy. LSU was good on both offense and defense. They won the Joe Moore Award for best offensive line, and the defense led the SEC in tackles.

LSU head coach Ed Orgeron* (center) *celebrates the LSU Tigers championship win over the Clemson Tigers.

The 2019 Tigers were led by head coach Ed Orgeron. He played defense at LSU in 1979. When he coached LSU from 2016 to 2021, 12 of his players were first-team All-Americans and four won national awards. He won several national Coach of the Year awards in 2019.

LSU TIGERS FACTS

- One of LSU's biggest rivals is Alabama. Nick Saban coached at LSU from 2000 to 2004. Then he coached at Alabama from 2007 until he retired in 2024.
- LSU won national titles in 1958, 2003, 2007, and 2019.
- Several LSU Tigers have had great careers on NFL teams. They include Odel Beckham Jr., Joe Burrow, Tyrann Mathieu, and Justin Jefferson.
- LSU has had 33 head coaches since the team started in 1893. In addition to Orgeron, three have led the team to national titles. Paul Ditzel did it in 1958, Nick Saban in 2003, and Les Miles in 2007.

Deshaun Watson was one of Clemson's best quarterbacks of all time.

NO. 9

Clemson University

Clemson University has won three national titles. The last two title-winning teams, the 2016 and 2018 Clemson Tigers, were led by great quarterbacks. In 2016, it was Deshaun Watson leading the way in the title game. Watson completed 36 of 42 passes to gain 420 yards. He threw three touchdown passes and no interceptions. His game-winning touchdown sealed the deal in a rematch against Alabama.

Trevor Lawrence was the quarterback for the 2018 national title. The Tigers were the first major college football team to finish with a record of 15–0 since 1897. This was the team's sixth undefeated season! They knocked out Notre Dame in the Cotton Bowl. The Tigers also won their fourth conference title in a row in an Atlantic Coast Conference game against the University of Pittsburgh.

Head coach Dabo Swinney has led the team since 2008. With a winning record of 80–7, he was ranked the fifth best coach in college football by *Sports Illustrated*.

Quarterback Trevor Lawrence runs with the ball in the 2018 Cotton Bowl game against Notre Dame.

CLEMSON TIGERS FACTS

- It's tough to beat Clemson on its home field. Opponents have nicknamed Clemson's Memorial Stadium "Death Valley."
- John Heisman coached football and baseball at Clemson from 1900 to 1903. The Heisman Trophy is named after him.
- Thirty-nine Tigers have been NFL first-round draft picks, including Nate Wiggins in 2024.
- Clemson plays rival South Carolina in the Palmetto Bowl every year. Clemson has won the game 73 times and lost 44 times.

NO. 8

Texas quarterback Vince Young heads for the end zone to score the winning touchdown in the 2006 Rose Bowl.

UNIVERSITY OF TEXAS

With more than 900 wins, the University of Texas is fourth on the all-time wins list in college football. The Texas Longhorns have won four national titles and 33 conference titles. The team has had 100 first-team All-Americans. Players Earl Campbell and Vince Young were honored with Heisman Trophy wins.

The 2005 team stands out in a big way. The Longhorns not only won the Big 12 Conference title game, they won it by the biggest margin ever. Their 70–3 victory over the University of Colorado was a blowout! The Longhorns finished the season 15–0 and won the national title.

Their 2006 Rose Bowl matchup against the University of Southern California was so exciting that ESPN called it one of the best games in college football history. Texas won the game when quarterback Vince Young made a rushing touchdown and a two-point conversion in the game's final seconds. It was the most-watched college football game ever with 35.6 million viewers.

Texas defender Michael Huff* (left) *forces a fumble against the Colorado Buffaloes in the 2005 Big 12 championship game.

TEXAS LONGHORNS FACTS

- The Longhorns are known for filling one of the largest stadiums in college football with excited fans. Texas Memorial Stadium seats more than 100,000 people and is often sold out for games.
- Texas won the national title in 1963, 1969, 1970, and 2005.
- The Longhorns have been rivals with Oklahoma State University since 1929. The Cotton Bowl is the scene of their yearly Red River Showdown. It is one the biggest games of the season for both teams.
- Quarterback Arch Manning joined the Longhorns in 2023. He is the nephew of famous NFL quarterbacks Eli and Peyton Manning.

NO. 7

Running back Herschel Walker carries the ball for Georgia against Notre Dame during the 1981 Sugar Bowl game.

UNIVERSITY OF GEORGIA

It was halftime at the 1980 SEC football championship. The University of Georgia Bulldogs were playing against rival Auburn. Georgia was down 15–2.

Bulldogs head coach Vince Dooley sent in backup running back Herschel Walker. Walker rushed 27 times in the second half for 84 yards. One 18-yard run resulted in a touchdown. Georgia won 31–21! Walker rushed for more than 5,000 yards in his

Georgia career and won the 1982 Heisman.

Good coaching, top talent, and a strong defense are the secrets of Georgia's success. The Bulldogs are known for a fast and physical defense. It was on full display in the 2022 national title game. Some football experts say it was the best defensive matchup in college football history. Georgia beat Alabama 33–18.

Georgia defenders celebrate a big play in 2021. That season, the Bulldogs won their first national title in more than 40 years.

In addition to four national titles, Georgia has 16 conference titles. The Bulldogs have also played in 62 bowl games. Their 38 victories make them number two in bowl game wins, behind Alabama's 45.

GEORGIA BULLDOGS FACTS

- The Georgia Bulldogs have been playing football since 1892.
- The Bulldogs won national titles in 1942, 1980, 2021, and 2022.
- Top Georgia running backs Frank Sinkwich and Hershel Walker were awarded Heisman Trophies.
- There were 58 former Bulldogs playing in the NFL in the 2024 season.

NO. 6

Nebraska fullback Jeff Makovicka **(left)** *makes a play against Michigan State during Nebraska's undefeated season in 1995.*

UNIVERSITY OF NEBRASKA

The University of Nebraska Cornhuskers were college football champs in 1970, 1971, 1994, 1995, and 1997. Their 1995 season was the best of all. The team was undefeated, and they outscored their opponents 638–201.

This wasn't the first time the Cornhuskers had an undefeated season. Between 1900 and 1916, they had five. They also set a team record by winning 34 games in a row from 1912 to 1916. The Cornhuskers have won the Big Ten Conference title 46 times.

Nebraska has been led by 31 head coaches since the football program started in 1890. Two coaches really stand out. Bob Devaney coached from 1957 to 1972. His assistant, Tom Osborne, took over in 1973. He coached until 1997. Both coaches won at least 100 games with Nebraska. Matt Rhule took over the team in 2023 and is working hard to bring a sixth national title to the school.

Nebraska quarterback Dylan Raiola hands the ball to running back Emmett Johnson in a 2024 game against Ohio State.

NEBRASKA CORNHUSKERS FACTS

- Three Nebraska superstars have been awarded Heisman Trophies: Johnny Rodgers, Mike Rozier, and Eric Crouch.
- Every Nebraska home game since 1962 has been sold out. Fans at Memorial Stadium chant "Husker Power" before the players come onto the field.
- They have played in 53 bowl games, including 35 straight from 1969 to 2003. That's an NCAA record.
- Seven Nebraska head coaches are in the College Football Hall of Fame: Edward Robinson, Fielding Yost, Dana Bible, Biff Jones, Bob Devaney, Tom Osborne, and Frank Solich.

NO. 5

Oklahoma quarterback Baker Mayfield runs with the ball in 2015.

UNIVERSITY OF OKLAHOMA

The University of Oklahoma's winning ways start with seven NCAA titles. The team's success is due to amazing players, including 167 All-Americans and seven Heisman Trophy winners. Outstanding coaches such as Bud Wilkinson, Barry Switzer, and Bob Stoops kept the victories coming.

The Oklahoma Sooners are known for their high-scoring offense. They ran over the University of Colorado in 1980 with a final score of 82–42. In 2003, they shut out Texas A&M and scored 77 points. Four years later, they clobbered the University of North Texas in the season-opener by a score of 79–10.

Quarterback Chandler Morris* (right) *helped lead the Sooners to their sixth Big 12 title in a row with a touchdown against the Iowa State Cyclones.

The Sooners made college football history with a 47-game winning streak that lasted from 1953 to 1957. They also have the most Big 12 Conference titles with 14. That includes six in a row from 2015 to 2020.

OKLAHOMA SOONERS FACTS

- A 1919 game against Kingfisher College was Oklahoma's most lopsided victory. The final score was 179–0.
- The NFL has drafted 417 Oklahoma players since the first draft in 1936.
- In 2017, quarterback Baker Mayfield led the team to a Big 12 record of 8,114 yards gained in the season.
- Heisman Trophy winner Sam Bradford was Oklahoma's quarterback in 2008. The Sooners scored 716 points to set a Big 12 record.

NO. 4

Head Coach Urban Meyer* (front row center) *brought the the Ohio State Buckeyes back from a losing season in 2011 to an undefeated season in 2012.

Ohio State University

Powerhouse is a word that's often used to describe Ohio State University football. They have won 39 Big Ten Conference titles and nine NCAA titles. They've had 10 undefeated seasons.

Coach Urban Meyer took over the Ohio State Buckeyes in 2012 after their first losing season since 1988. His goal was to make Ohio State a powerhouse again. He led the team to an undefeated 12–0 season. During Meyer's seven years with the team, they never lost more than two games in a season.

Meyer set up a winning culture at Ohio State that continues to this day. Since coach Ryan Day took over in 2019, he has led the team to a 56–8 record. This includes winning 39 out of 42 games against other Big Ten teams. It also includes a Sugar Bowl win in 2020, a Rose Bowl win in 2021, and the national title in 2024.

Buckeyes wide receiver Garrett Wilson (right) catches a pass in a 56–7 win against Michigan in 2021.

OHIO STATE BUCKEYES FACTS

- The Buckeyes were national college football champs in 1942, 1954, 1957, 1961, 1968, 1970, 2002, 2014, and 2024.
- Ohio State running back Archie Griffin is the only player to win the Heisman Trophy twice. He won in 1974 and 1975.
- Ohio State's marching band gives a free concert for fans before every home game called the Skull Session. Fans pack St. John Arena to hear the band.
- Buckeyes who went on to become NFL stars include Chris Spielman, Ezekiel Elliott, and Chase Young.

NO. 3

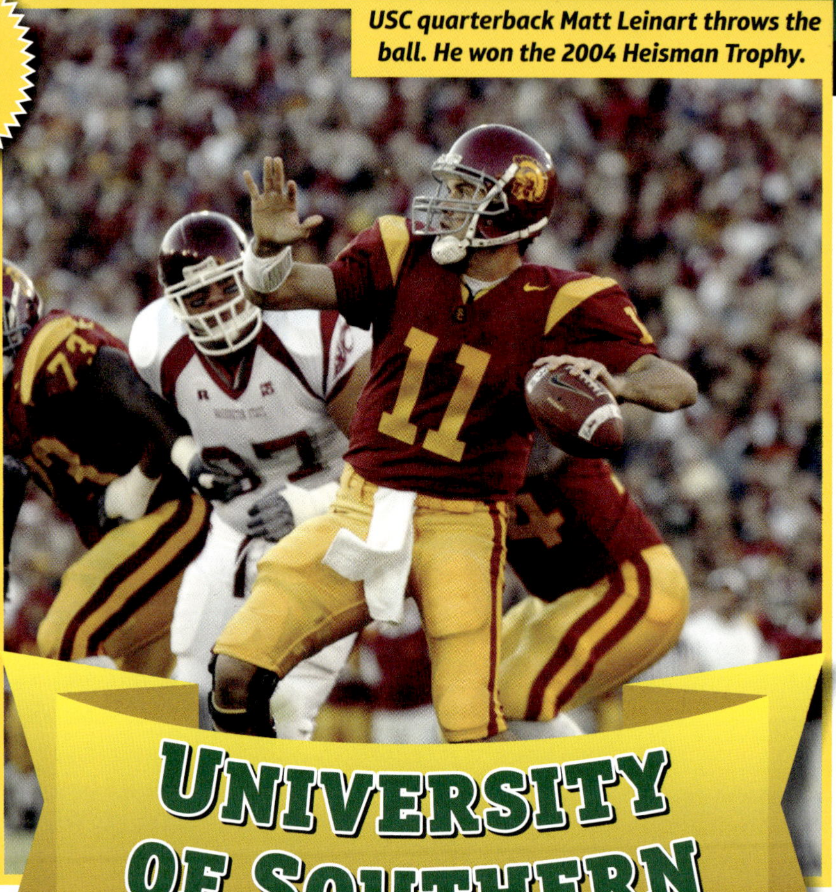

USC quarterback Matt Leinart throws the ball. He won the 2004 Heisman Trophy.

UNIVERSITY OF SOUTHERN CALIFORNIA

The USC Trojans have been crowned national champs 11 times. Of those big wins, their 2004 title was the most impressive. Pete Carroll coached Heisman Trophy-winner Matt Leinart at quarterback. The team's motto that year was "Leave No Doubt."

In 2004, the undefeated Trojans met the unbeaten Oklahoma Sooners for the title. Leinart threw a record-breaking five touchdowns. USC's 55–19 victory left no doubt about who was the better team.

Winning is something USC does often. Since their first season in 1888, the Trojans have an overall record of 874 wins, 374 losses, and 54 ties. They've had 13 undefeated seasons and 37 Pac-10 Conference titles.

Record-breaking USC quarterback Caleb Williams* (right) *runs for a touchdown against Notre Dame in 2022.

Quarterback Caleb Williams came from Oklahoma to play for USC in 2022. Williams threw a national record-breaking 42 touchdowns and 3,333 yards. He also won the Heisman Trophy that year.

USC TROJANS FACTS

- In 1928, the Trojans were unbeaten and won their first national title. They outscored opposing teams 207–59.
- USC has played in 34 Rose Bowl games. The Trojans have won 25 times.
- At least one Trojan player has been chosen in the NFL draft for a record-breaking 70 years in a row.
- The winningest head coach in USC history is John McKay with 127 wins.

NO. 2

Wide receiver Anthony Carter makes a touchdown catch for the Michigan Wolverines in 1982.

UNIVERSITY OF MICHIGAN

In 1979, the University of Michigan Wolverines were up against the University of Indiana. With six seconds left in the game, the score was tied. Michigan quarterback John Wanger sent a 45-yard pass sailing into the end zone. Freshman wide receiver Anthony Carter was waiting to catch it and claim a game-winning touchdown. Michigan won 27–21. Wolverines fans remember this fantastic play as the Michigan Miracle.

Michigan Wolverines head coach Jim Harbaugh holds the title trophy after a 34–13 win against the University of Washington.

The University of Michigan football team has the most wins in college history. The Wolverines have 1,012 wins since their first season in 1879. They have racked up 12 national titles and 45 Big Ten Conference titles. They regularly fill the nation's largest college football stadium with more than 100,000 fans.

In 2023, the Wolverines beat the University of Washington Huskies for the national title. The Wolverines crushed the Huskies 34–13. It was Michigan's first undefeated season in 25 years.

MICHIGAN WOLVERINES FACTS

- In 1902, Michigan won the first Rose Bowl game ever played. They shut out Stanford University 49–0.
- Gerald Ford was US president from 1974 to 1977. He played center for the Wolverines and was voted the most valuable player on the 1934 team.
- Former NFL superstar Tom Brady had a 20–5 record when he was Michigan's starting quarterback in 1998 and 1999.
- Michigan's rivalry with Ohio State University is fierce. The teams have met 120 times since 1897. Michigan leads with 62 victories, 51 losses, and six ties.

NO. 1

Head coach Nick Saban led Alabama to six national titles.

UNIVERSITY OF ALABAMA

The University of Alabama Crimson Tide tops this G.O.A.T. list. The team has won 18 national titles. Alabama has been led by amazing players and two of the greatest coaches in college football history.

Bear Bryant was head coach at Alabama for 25 years, from 1958 to 1982. During that time, the Crimson Tide won six national titles. By the time Bryant retired, he had led the team to 323 wins. This was more wins than any other college coach.

Head coach Nick Saban took over in 2007. Saban led the team to six more NCAA titles. Alabama had been going through a down period when he took over. But in his second season, they finished with a perfect 12–0 record.

Alabama quarterback Tua Tagovailoa tries to keep the ball away from an LSU player in 2019.

Some of Alabama's very best players have also had successful careers in the NFL. They include quarterbacks Bart Starr, Joe Namath, Bryce Young, and Tua Tagovailoa. Other great players are tight end Ozzie Newsome and wide receiver DeVonta Smith.

ALABAMA CRIMSON TIDE FACTS

- Head coach Wallace Wade led the 1930 team to an undefeated 10–0 season, including eight shutouts.
- Alabama has had many great players. But none won the Heisman Trophy until 2009. Running back Mark Ingram claimed the award after his team had an undefeated season.
- Alabama's all-time record is 988 wins, 315 losses, and 42 ties.
- The Crimson Tide has played in 76 bowl games, more than any other team. They also have the most wins at 45.

YOUR G.O.A.T.

It's your turn to put together your own list of G.O.A.T. college football teams. Which ones make your fantasy football lineup? Which teams do you cheer on during Saturday afternoon games? What stats and facts impress you the most?

The teams in this book have stood out from the pack with star players, great coaches, and big wins. They have been consistent for many seasons.

It's time to grab a pen and a sheet of paper and make your own G.O.A.T. list. Do any of your picks match the teams in this book? It's your list. You decide!

COLLEGE FOOTBALL FACTS

- On November 6, 1869, Rutgers University and Princeton University played the first college football game. Rutgers won 6–4. At the time, the game looked a lot different than it does now. Players were not allowed to carry or throw the ball. They could only bat it with their hands, feet, heads, and bodies.

- The Army versus Navy game is one of the biggest rivalries in college football history. The games have been played between the US Military Academy and the US Naval Academy since 1890. Navy has won 62 games and Army 55, with seven ties.

- The biggest blowout in college football history was between Georgia Tech and Cumberland College in 1916. Georgia won by a score of 222–0.

GLOSSARY

bowl game: a special game played after the regular season

conference: a group of teams that play against one another

draft: when teams take turns choosing new players

Heisman Trophy: an award given every year to the best college football player

National Collegiate Athletic Association (NCAA): the group that oversees college sports in the United States

roster: a list of players on a team

rush: to advance the football with running plays

scholarship: money given to a student to help pay for school

title: championship

two-point conversion: a play after a touchdown that scores two points if it is successful

LEARN MORE

Adelman, Beth. *G.O.A.T. College Football Players*. Minneapolis, Lerner Publications, 2026.

Doeden, Matt. *34 Amazing Facts About Football.* Minneapolis: Lerner Publications, 2024.

Ducksters: College Football and the BCS
https://www.ducksters.com/sports/college_football.php

Heisman Trophy Winners
https://www.heisman.com/heisman-winners

NCAA: Football
https://www.ncaa.com/sports/football/fbs

Streeter, Anthony. *College Football Championship All-Time Greats.* Mendota Heights, MN: Press Box Books, 2025.

INDEX

PHOTO ACKNOWLEDGMENTS

Photo Credits: Interior; EFKS/Shutterstock, interior; Mtsaride/Shutterstock, interior; robertsrob/ iStockphoto, interior; Yummybuum/Shutterstock, interior; Alex Voylokov/ Shutterstock, p. 4; Neil Leifer/Getty, p. 5; Mike Ehrman/Getty, p. 6; Tim Warner/ Getty, p. 8; University Images/Getty, p. 9; Alika Jenner/Getty, p. 10; Tyler Smith/ Getty, p. 11; Tom Pennington/Getty, p. 12; Fort Worth Star-Telegram/Getty, p. 13; G. N. Lawrence/Getty, p. 14; Focus on Sport/Getty, p. 15; Todd Kirkland/Getty, p. 16; Matthew Stockman/Getty, p. 17; Jason Mowry/Getty, p. 18; Brett Deering/Getty, p. 19; Tom Pennington/Getty, p. 20; Jamie Sabau/Getty, p. 21; Mike Mulholland/Getty, p. 22; Robert Beck/Getty, p. 23; Ronald Martinez/Getty, p. 24; Carl Skalak/Getty; p. 25; Houston Chronicle/Hearst Newspapers/Getty, p. 26; Kevin C. Cox/Getty, p. 27, Todd Kirland/Getty.

Cover: Todd Rosenberg/AP